A
LIGHT
DUSTING
OF
BREATH

Donna Pucciani

ISBN: 978-0-944048-61-0

purple flag press online at vacpoetry.org/purple-flag
Design & front cover image by forgetgutenberg.com
Back cover image from www.flickr.com/photos/ef-
lon/5176771319/

ACKNOWLEDGEMENTS

The following poems have previously appeared in some form in the publications below:

"Recollected" in JAMA; "Planetary" in *Coffee House*; "Envy" and "The Girls of St. Hilda's" in *After Hours*; "Siblings" in *DuPage Valley Review*; "Southern Comfort" in *Chaffin*; "Thumb Tricks" in *The Alembic*; "Last Journey" in *After Hours* and *New Laurel Review*; "Scattering the Parents" in *Off the Coast*; "Doctor" in *The Cape Rock*; "Teachers" in *America*; "Italian Tutorial" in *Atlanta Review*; "Muti's Left Hand" in *Briar Cliff Review* and *Bloodroot*; "At the Movies" in *Journal*; "Night Wear" in *After Hours*; "Opening the Curtains" in *The Cape Rock*; "The Cranes" in *Soundings East*; "Conjecture" in *Amoskeag*; "Red Canal, Berlin" in *The Wonderbook of Poetry* and *Colere*; "Canal, Berlin" in *Turtle Island*; "Bonnie's Street" in *The Wonderbook of Poetry* and *Pennsylvania English*; "Facade, Berlin" in *Pennsylvania English*; "WinterWillow Graffiti" in *The Wonderbook of Poetry*; "While waiting" in *America*; "Languages" in *North Dakota Quarterly*; "Reunion" in *Pennine Ink*; "Goodbyes" in *Istanbul Literary Review*; "The Memory" in *North Dakota Quarterly*; "Lines to Gregory Corso," "Letter from Italy," and "Outside Rome" in *PoetryMagazine.com*; "At the Protestant Cemetery" in *Feile-Festa* and *Paterson Literary Review*; "Going to Paris" in *Urthona Magazine*; "Varda, Hungary" in *Jabberwock* and *Stand*; "The Cousins' Visit" in *Acumen* and *Pearl*; "Easter 2013, Scotland" in *Cold Mountain Review*; "Murder at the Palace Theatre" and "Living Room" in *Pennine Ink*; "Mortality" in *Home Planet News*; "Smoke" in JAMA; "Advent" in *The Wonderbook of Poetry* and *The Christian Century*; "god is" in *Cairn*; "notes to god" in *Third Wednesday*; "Still" in *Feile-Festa* and *North Dakota Review*; "Quiet House" in *Prairie Winds, Summerset Review, Willow Review*; "Bells" in JAMA and *Hildegard von Bingen: An Inspiration*, ed. Gabriel Griffin, Isola San Giulio: Wyvern Works, 2014; "Bodycolour" in *Chautauqua Review* and *After Hours*; "Reading Garcia Lorca in Italian" in *After Hours*; "See-Saw at Dusk" in *Taj Mahal*; "Sidewalk and Ball" in *The Wonderbook of Poetry*; "Saxophone Quartet" in *Gihon River Review*; "Piccolo" and "How Things Go" in *Seems*; "Only Connect" in *Cairn*; "At the Museum" in *Gihon River Review*; "Sleep" in *The Alembic*; "The Pines" in *Dream Catcher*; "Extinction" in *Off the Coast*; "Mountain and Lake" in *Quantum Leap*; "Summer's Lease" in *Cairn* and *Briar Cliff Review*; "Hedges" in *Poetry East*; "The Long Hill" and "River" in *Journal*; "Stormy" in *Plainsongs*; "Storm after Drought" in *After Hours*; "Aftermath" in *Plainsongs*; "Fallen" in *PoetryMagazine.com*; "Rockery" in *Pulsar Webzine*; "Dahlias" in *The New Writer*; "Robin" in *Front Range Review*; "Noncommittal" in *After Hours*; "Grapes" and "The secret of stillness" in *Summerset Review*; "Only because" in *Acumen*. Some of the above poems, including those set in Berlin, have appeared on Shutterverse2.wordpress.com, a collaborative website featuring the work of Boston/Berlin-based artist/photographer X Bonnie Woods.

Thanks to Steven Schroeder and Purple Flag Press for making this book possible.

For Peter

CONTENTS

PART I: *Dramatis Personae*

PART II: *"somewhere i have never travelled"*

PART III: *Objects of Desire*

PART IV: *Lost Habitat*

PART I

Dramatis Personae

Recollected

The photos emerge
from their hiding place in the cellar,

sepia fish, or paper ghosts
with white deckled borders.

Our fathers, long dead, boast
the cheerful sibilance of baldness,

a halo in the camera's flash.
Our mothers, bedecked

in aprons and strange eyeglasses,
flap like crows' wings.

Then ourselves, in jeans too tight
or loose, a scherzo of lapels

and weird hair. It hurts to laugh
at our remembered youth.

Take the day Grandma
sprayed her hair with starch.

We cleaned her up, then piled into
the Studebaker for New Year's fireworks.

Dolor squeezes through the cracks
of memory—the career that never was,

the shock of suicide. In the blur
of work, food, sleep, we sigh

platitudes: we have our health,
we have each other,

knowing that even these gifts
will be snatched from our hands

as if we were children wanting too much.
Our ration, randomly appointed,

is an orange in a stocking
hung on the mantel for Christmas.

Planetary

My planet passes the sun every year
on the date of my birth at Garfield Memorial,
a hospital in D.C. that no longer exists. But I still exist,
having squirmed my way out of my mother's legs
into the gloved hands of Dr. Caroline Jackson, I'm told,
after a fifteen-minute interval in which
they discovered we were twins.

Today, however, is much like any other day.
I get up early, walk, shower, eat a sensible breakfast,
and sit at my desk to work. But first, I open cards.

From two thousand miles away
my twin sister's salutation arrives.
My mirror image shifts from Arizona,
where she sends wishes through desert and monsoon
to my black metal mailbox on a shady curb
in suburban Chicago.

Sixty revolutions around our star.
Despite our closeness in the womb,
two different slippery-blue umbilicals
have slid us into a separate space.

The dictates of a sundial on some unyielding rock,
or a clock that flashes minutes into distances,
have replaced the power of touch. Our voices
subsist on a cup of coffee, a monitor,
a fragment of paper set smiling on the bookcase.

Envy

I often visited them when I was a child,
those families with a cabin on a lake,
amazed that people could have two houses,
one for winter, one for summer, people
who annually moved from one to the other
the way I changed shoes for sandals.

No locks on the doors, no carpets
on the wooden floors, only oval rag rugs
twisted by hand from some aunt
who had owned the place years ago
and graciously left it behind.

My friends spent their Junes
learning how to glide a canoe.
They hopped as easily from boat
to pier as I hop-scotched on a sidewalk,
chalk in one hand, skate key in the other.

They ran barefoot for months,
their browned bodies smelling
of fresh air and pines, or shriveled
from hours in a lake gleaming blue.

Then, wrapped in colored towels,
their hair still wet, their freckles multiplied
by the sun, they giggled at television sit-coms
and dropped popcorn on the sofa.

My house was hot and dark,
mother, as always, under the weather,
while I sat in my bedroom under the eaves
learning to love the feel of a book.

The Girls of St. Hilda's

Comforting, somehow,
Liz describes the class reunion.
Every year, school chums
gather like blackbirds in a tree,
singing for just one day
in a far corner of England.

The rest of the year, their faces
float like star dancers
among geraniums and folded socks,
hover like apples at the lip of a bowl,
drift like clouds in a crocodile sky.

Memories are silvery things.
They arrive at the hour of the traces
like little shells, bird skulls,
bits of straw, the puffed gills
of fish, a knife lodged in bread.

Once, everything was possible.
Then one spring, the smell of earth
was stronger than before, the scent
of lengthening shadows darker,
the irrevocable order of events
finally visible in the setting sun.

The children have left home,
husbands have died or play golf for escape.
The old scholars in pearls
have learned to be alone,
to make art from catastrophe,
traveling infinite distances every year
back into each others' arms,
sitting again at wooden desks with inkwells
among walls painted brown and cream,
then sipping strong tea and sherry in the parlour.

The sleeves of their cashmere sweaters
brush the tops of pastries, the watercress memories,
the trays of crust-less sandwiches
garnished with cucumber smiles.

Siblings

It usually happens at weddings and funerals,
or at the end of life
when all should be tranquil.
Instead, the stitch of anger
slips through the loosened loop of time,
unraveling family ties.

Who should or should not have appeared
assumes great importance. The presence
of somebody's brother at the church,
the absence of sister at the funeral,
makes the air above the coffin burn
with incendiary glances.

A bride's veil stiffens imperceptibly,
her white bouquet of lilies and baby's breath
shivers under the invisible stares of the uninvited.

Suddenly nobody remembers Thanksgiving,
when the cousins were always late and the gravy
thin, but life went on among the mashed potatoes.
Dad carved the bird, the aunties split
the wishbone, and everyone clapped.

There's a picture of children making mud-pies
in the shadow of a backyard fence. Here's one
of a girl dressed as Annie Oakley. Her brother
has loaned her his holster, his plastic gun.

Now it's imperative to hunch one's shoulders
at the wake, cursing the one who signed the papers for
"the manor," after Mama was found wandering the streets
under the querulous gaze of the moon.
Or somebody's first wife was seated well behind
the family, her humiliation flickering like
a thousand candles setting the church ablaze.

The rancors of the dead are pulverized
along with their bodies, but the living
exchange acerbities that rise through the trees
like a plague of locusts, leaving behind
the tattered lace of bitter tongues.

Southern Comfort

The cousins down south are hospitable,
wear T-shirts that read *Laissez les bontemps rouler*,
bring up children who call us "ma'am" and "sir,"
believe Jesus died for their sins.

In dreams of childhood,
we chase mosquito trucks down the street,
reveling in misted poison.

We catch frogs in tin buckets,
help Grandma patch the screen door
with cotton balls.

The long, slow evenings fill
with crickets and humidity.
We dab bug bites with calamine lotion,
watch old Westerns on television.

We create ourselves anew each night,
bathed and night-gowned, sipping root beer floats
on the porch under an orange moon,
counting pink polka-dots on skinny legs,

as now we watch a penny-candy sunset
with guilty pleasure, listening for
the somnolent song of locusts in the night.

Thumb Tricks

Why, on a winter's night
in Chicago, should I suddenly
remember my grandmother's thumb,
how she could curl it back
to practically touch her wrist?

As a child, after tweezing her whiskers
from the throne of her magnanimous lap,
I'd watch her display her magical thumb,
curled like the crescent of the tropical moon
over Aunt Betty's greenhouse,
or the swanlike necks of the orchids within.

And when she whistled for us, that same
thumb bent towards her forefinger,
making a charmed circlet that she held
between pursed lips. At the shriek,
we'd come running down the block,
pigtails flying, while gumbo
bubbled on the stove.

Later, lying alone on my bed
in the dark humidity of New Orleans,
I'd try to close my lips around my fingers
to recreate the sharp call to dinner,
emitting not sound but saliva. Then,
seeking at the sill the moon's small scythe
cutting the sky over Lake Pontchartrain,
I'd attempt her other trick, pushing
my thumb painfully out and down,

my childish brain wondering
how hands behave, fingers bend,
bodies move or do not move
as we would wish, nor minds nor tongues.

Last Journey

Mother and Daddy bump down the Interstate
in the trunk of a silver Toyota
speeding through Hattiesburg, Mississippi.
Their ashes slept last night
in a star-smitten Memphis
after dinner at the Catfish Cabin
eight hours south of Chicago.

They'd grown tired of the cellar
in a suburban bungalow west of Lake Michigan,
where their whispers had limped and listed
in the silent damp, now summer-sodden,
now spangled in an aura of snow.
It was time to go

back where they came from,
scattered on the levee or Lake Pontchartrain,
where Brother Jimmy of the local church
had offered to "say a few words,"
which we'd have refused because the deceased
never did "find Jesus."

But years ago, angels and devils were sent
to round up Lieutenant Frank giving kindly orders
to Italian POWs, and Lucile at the Army
printing office, for a marriage, part miracle,
part nightmare.

Half a century later, in a daughter's basement,
they found a restless peace from cancer and dementia
atop a chest of old candles, gift wrap, and maps,
watching laundry pass through the hands
of the living, listening to their tired footsteps
on the stairs.

Now the road through burned-up cornfields
leads from Illinois to Missouri, Arkansas
down to the Crescent River whose mouth awaits them,
their bones turning the Delta
a paler shade of brown.

Scattering the Parents

Mother's ashes take the wind
on the levee, in back of a plantation
where she'd love to have played
the lady of the manor, a nouveau-
Scarlett, with her long hair
trailing like moss through the live oaks.
Her bones mist the air
over the spiral staircase of her dreams.

Father's dust mingles with hers
on the Mississippi shoreline,
cast from the high earthen border
built to withstand wind and water,
but, in fact, fallible.

Dad, as in life, is hesitant, circumspect.
The wind dies down at our backs,
and clumps that were once
his dark hair, full mouth, and tennis elbow,
hit the shoreline with a thud, drifting
after mother's white magnolia gown,
with water lapping what used to be
their toes.

Doctor

for Vivek Talwar, M.D.

The way he held you,
laid you back on the examination table
slowly, like a mother cribside

putting the baby down for a nap,
made something new happen.
You had been dizzy with a vertigo

that had no name, no passage
except the spinning, which,
even reclining, made you feel

like a bird falling from the nest.
But this particular doctor,
a man of science, a scholar

of anatomy, physiology,
and the biochemistry of pain
in all its forms, summoned

a different knowledge,
voiced aloud a charm stronger
than any wizardry of nature

or breadth of genius,
his sentence succinct:
Don't be afraid, I've got you.

Teachers

I feel lighter now,
as though I have lost body parts
one by one, watching them
sink like stones in a lake,
or drift into the garden of sky.

Each mentor's mortality came to visit
and refused to leave. Old music teachers,
philosophy profs, a poet-friend,
died of cancer, dementia, flu,
a windmill of maladies that lifted them
into the air, then dropped them
unceremoniously into death.

Each one is a phantom limb,
made of flesh, bone, and blood.
One a shoulder, another a leg
for climbing mountains, another
a hand for stretching octaves,
a mind for wrapping intellect
in the unlikely bonds of compassion,
a talent for birthing conversation
in all-night cafés.

They dwelt in harpsichords,
telescopes, and tomes.
The slow moon overhead
canonizes them, bestows haloes
visible only to me.

Italian Tutorial

Three pupils gather at the table,
arranging their books. They ignore
the snow falling outside the library,
the grey sky lowering,
the wind slicing the parking lot,
toothpick students running,

and imagine themselves in Venice,
or the Coliseum consumed by lions,
or a small *ristorante* in the Alps eating
tortellini filled with improbable pumpkin.

The tutor's voice smoothes out
their misshapen vowels, calms
their anxious verbs with just the right
endings, placing them on their tongues
as communion.

They chant conjugations
like the monks of Monte Cassino,
scribbling illuminations in primary colors.
Their ritual words rise like incense
as they receive the sacrament of the *imperfetto*,
humbled by their own imperfection,
their sluggish phrases mired
in flawed memory.

The air is heavy with the act of thinking,
the burden of pronouns.
Two hours later, they finish,
calling good-byes in their borrowed language,
craving the grace of fluency,
holding notebooks like benedictions.

Muti's Left Hand

For Riccardo Muti
and the Chicago Symphony

His right hand gives the downbeat
with the stick. The opening chords
rise into the chandelier netted
with lights and microphones.

Like a bird escaping its cage,
his left hand flutters out from his lapel,
then grasps his heart to keep it
from bursting. He lets it go,
a gull diving over a sea of violins
into the deep bell of the tuba.

Wait. Be still. I'll tell you when.
He does so, punching *sforzando*
with a left hook, then flinging in a handful
of salt, seasoning soup as his grandmother did.
He knows how to simmer.

Palm upturned, he welcomes woodwinds,
shakes the open hand next to his chest,
strumming an invisible lute. Now leaning,
he points like an angry father, reproaching
the violas. Paw becomes claw, casting a spell
on the horns. Then fingers point up,
like Holman Hunt's Jesus in the Doorway.

Brahms' Second is long and he is tired.
He needs to rest that left hand. Tonight,
if he sleeps on his back, it will recline
on the blanket or crawl beneath it.
If he's on his stomach, he will tuck it
under his pillow to keep it still. If
on his side, it will cradle his head
to catch leftover themes.

Crouching, he turns the page, nods to the flutes,
smiles a crooked smile at the oboes, and
flicks his wrist at the brass: *Run with it.*

At the Movies

Today we sit in the dark,
thigh to thigh. Popcorn butters us
with its ubiquitous embrace.

Will today bring intrigue in Russia,
gondolas in Venice gliding under
the Bridge of Sighs, or planets
crashing in space?

The murmur of expectation ebbs
as we pass the hours in the flicker
of miracles, tragedies, other lives.
Music blooms with every kiss.

I am suddenly grateful to God or the Fates
for whatever they had imagined for us,
to have lived together unremarkably
in modest, well-lit rooms
for three decades and more.

Afterwards, blinking, we shamble out
to the old car with dents inflicted
by careless drivers over the years,
or by hailstorms, and slide back

into our small, precious life,
its secrets and flights, real and fanciful,
revealed in the early snow that fogs
the windows with our light dusting of breath.

Night Wear

He's taken to wearing colors to bed,
orange tees, or eggplant, the new purple,

with boxer shorts in mismatched plaids.
Is he planning to woo me all over again,

replacing his worn-out stripes
that button down the front, the vee

having humbly framed his fleshy neck
for years? His old sheepskin moccasins

have fallen apart, the stitching frayed
like the wicks of spent candles.

He now wears dark, smooth slip-ons,
and floats about the house

before bedtime like a well-shod
aristocrat. Finally, sitting on the edge

of the bed, he swivels free of leather,
then cotton. Mischief, autumn,

and jazz rise from the crooked
little toe on his right foot.

The crickets are singing
their song of summer

to young minds in old skins.
The moon opens wide,

welcoming the dark
with bright silk.

Opening the Curtains

In the division of labor
that is marriage, one of his daily jobs,
assumed for no particular reason,
is to open the curtains. Each morning,
wandering from one room to the next,
he lets in the sky, enjoying the pull
of the cords, the vision of cloud,
rain, or new snow, framed in
the crossword design of windows.

The sudden rush of light opens
our small domicile to the air,
making the old carpets smile,
the worn sofa sit up a little straighter,
making mother's dining room table shine
through morning motes.

Today he watches the chipmunks
that have tunneled under the steps,
the potted petunias sunning themselves,
a passing garbage truck
marking the dawn's departure.

He is reminded
that he can still pad barefoot
among the airy little rooms,
gathering the night's quiet
in the palm of a hand, tugging his
grateful dailiness from the rhythmic
swing of the pleated fabric,
from the rope's rough whisper.

The Cranes

We've met, by chance, some friends,
an elderly couple, he smiling,
she wide-eyed with dementia,
strolling the path through wood
and meadow. They cry, *Look!*
The cranes, overhead!
Fifty or a hundred commas
gather in the sky as if
they do not know to what sentence
they currently belong, and,
lacking syntax, wander so high
as to be almost invisible.

Some mysterious compass
calls them away in the mindless
pilgrimage of migration. They trill
among themselves, their bustles
and bills catching a silver sun,
tell stories of God and humankind
to the stratus and the open sedge-
meadows below. Sometimes
they remember their drooping
rump-feathers wagging in a courtship
dance, their grass-tossing, twig-playing
life in the wetlands.

The high-pitched lunacy
of their gargled laugh
lights up the forest below
that has all but lost its gold
in autumn's dizzying wind.
They dance as if sending
a message of great importance
which they themselves have forgotten
in the gradual vanishing
of their soaring, unflappable wings.

Conjecture

What if sun and moon
were to collide in space,
spawning sparks of gold and silver,
little gods and goddesses falling to earth
to make everything right?

The rich would turn their pockets inside out
for an old man shivering in a basement flat.
He needs warmth and bread,
but wants only his wife back. He has saved
her blue sweater from the hospital,
keeps it under his pillow, smells it
when he is too cold to sleep.

What if the eight women bombed yesterday
while gathering wood could return,
scarved and gossiping, arms full of twigs?
What if their broken children could be sewn up
like dolls, resurrected clean and desert-pink,
arms and legs where God put them, shrapnel
vanishing like light to bless an invisible sky?

What if truth popped like firecrackers
from the eyes of politicians, if bankers
ate of a golden fruit that made them
un-Midas their vast incredible coffers
for hospitals? What if the poor
had homes, shoes, books?

What if the four seasons
could follow a gentle sequence:
snow, blossom, leaf and warmth,
moderating all desire? Even if death
remains inevitable—what if
chrysanthemums of joy could fold us up
from our sickbeds as we slept, suck out
all breath before we knew what was happening,
to leave the living gasping in surprise, not grief,
holding a white flower to the heart?

PART II

"somewhere i have never travelled..."

—*e .e. cummings*

Red Canal
Berlin

The nightmare so unshakeable
descends even in daytime, subtle
as a dove: the canal below the window
brightens into blood, the banks
on both sides smeared with crimson mud.

Thirty years ago, a woman
stood at the kitchen window
looking out at a cluster of sparrows
and barbed wire. Her hands
were floury with the day's labors,
her heart heavy with hidden lives, lies,
the deaths of swimmers in the canal
at the hands of soldiers who used to be
her neighbors' children playing in the street.

Could she roll out death
like a pie, serve it for dessert,
with coffee and steamed milk
disguised as hope? And now,
how can she face the scarlet waters
coursing slowly through Berlin
with all the old invisible sadnesses
in tow?

Some day the canal will lighten
into pink. The landlocked night terrors
for those gone for a swim and then
to an early grave will subside,
leaving only whitewashed buildings,
windows sparkling with sunlight, geraniums,
and the pale faces of those who cannot endure
even the sparest of memories.

What will she do now
with the gift of a gunless life?

Canal, Berlin

Everyone thinks
this canal is just a canal,
the setting sun only a sun.
Passersby concern themselves
with dinner, grandchildren's birthdays,
walking small dogs in the park.

Everyone waits
for the memories to disappear
like burnt-off smog, like footsteps
left behind on the opposite bank.

They take care
not to catch their reflection
in the still water, not to find
the past in fingers of drifted twigs
or the wake of a distant boat.

Truth was the biggest casualty.
Those who sought to tell the tale
disappeared speechlessly into the night.

No blood sullies this water now,
no sign of guns or bloated flesh.
Eyes seek the blue of the sky,
not the pulse of despair,
not the lost years when East met West,
touched, but never joined.

Those who crossed,
perhaps survived and stayed,
stare across the mute canal,
bathe in the sacred shadow
of a crumbled wall
fragmented by souvenir hunters
who chipped away its somber dark
and pocketed the stones.

Bonnie's Street

The street awaits footsteps, bicycles, cars,
the vehicles of those who pursue loneliness
in continual transit.

Apartments link arms,
peer over a canal ringed with graffiti,
watch the intrusion of a small boat.

Someone on the fourth floor
sips wine, surveying cloud,
leaf and sky, watching

students with backpacks, a cyclist
turning a corner too quickly, an elderly soul
bent over a bag of cabbages for dinner.

In the distance, the hunched granite city
of Berlin crouches small as a fingernail,
or a cluster of berries visible

on this tree-lined street where window boxes
fringe the vacant eyes of flats,
the last vestige of warmth caught
in the arms of a red geranium.

Facade, Berlin

How many times a day
do footsteps cross the lintel
into city grit? Passersby
never see who comes and goes
from the rectangular niche
of a dark blue door,
or the graffiti that swaggers
across two-tone grey plaster,
where coral sills echo
the colors of earth and sky.

A woman with her hair pulled back,
a leather bag on her shoulder,
has never noticed the reluctant
collusion of carefully painted cottages,
now pitted and peeling,
or the swollen alphabets of youth.

At dawn the sparrows flit
under swags of dying lilac.
They watch who enters and exits
under the dried boughs. Together they sing
of pale purple, tender green,
and the bronze click of the latch.

WinterWillow Graffiti
Berlin

As if the snow that fell yesterday
were not thick enough, ready
to become slush over mud and under boots.

As if the cold were not cruel enough
to frost windows and the chilblained
elderly filling hot water bottles
and drinking endless cups of tea.

As if tortuous gusts would never cease
their insidious assault on cracked walls
and shuttered balconies.

What's left of the willow
waves listless over a concrete barrier,
whispers to the black-on-blue graffiti,

the crimson music notes
edging down the wall, thin green hearts
that once felt love, dribbled sea shells
that never knew a beach.

Looking for humanity and finding none,
the willow drifts yellow over a landscape
crammed with the violent creativity of the young,

whose bitter dreams
have claimed this corner
with a sprayed scream.

Too tired to think of Miami or Rio,
perhaps too old to remember spring,
the willow reaches down to pluck

a little of life, or anything,
from this grey winter afternoon,
seeking and finding new ways to weep.

While waiting

for the night, we decide
we must leave now
while we can.

New York is sinking.
We go to Pompeii, itself a reminder
that nothing is permanent.

Vesuvius erupted yesterday,
volcanic ash blanching
the air above Naples.

At the airport, we rent a car,
and suddenly we can smell
the sea, feel distended light.

We seek God in the vortex
of ocean and sand, find
grandmother's hills.

Twisted olive branches
twine with chestnuts
in the valley, arcing

to the sky. The disc of sun
falls from heaven
into the city of ghosts.

Like us, the horizon moves
but never really disappears.
We finish where the sky begins.

Languages

I have swallowed the seed of languages.
It grows in me like the tree
my mother promised me
when I swallowed the pips
in the orange juice.

Little words sprout like aliens,
spawning a jungle around themselves.
I will not speak English
in this country of sun and stone,

where the scent of tanned leather
bursts from the shops, and pasta
blooms inky black
with the blood of the squid.

On the tongue,
each day begins with bright vowels
buttering the dark crusty bread
of consonants.
Chew, savor, speak.

Reunion
Lago di Garda, Italy

How is it possible
that we from skyscrapers
and you from the mountain
have met in this cobbled alley
across the sea? Only the bells
keep track of time.

Our hands bloom in tongues,
our thoughts flutter like colored wings
alighting on each others' faces.

At lunch, you cut your trout carefully,
seeking bones in the snowy flesh.
I eat pizza with my hands, like a foreigner.
We drink coffee and grappa
as small sacraments.

These days everything surprises us.
We are alive, having avoided
the abyss for another year.
We've renewed our passports,
practiced Italian clichés, know
turbulence and backache.

We finally eat this simple meal,
able to swallow, dream, toast
the promise of a harvest moon.

Goodbyes

We'd stayed five days in the south,
pressed into mountains
and the impossibly blue Tyrrhenian.
At the Paola station, the family
carry our bags,
lift them onto the train
after kissing both cheeks,
which are suddenly wet.
The cousins line up
along the platform, their faces
a family portrait in the grimy
rectangle of window.

Rosetta, who says little
and cooks much, trembles.
The others smile, wave,
disappear as the train whistles
long and away.
We sway, settle in for the distance
north to Rome, eat sandwiches
of Parma ham. By now,

the *cugini* have turned
to walk back to the car,
drive among the hills
past the summer house on the sea,
past the hill of the monastery
with the river rushing alongside
the cloister, where Padre Ernesto
prays for us all, seeing everything
with his one good eye.

The Memory

The coffee here is strong and hot.
Seagulls have rediscovered the piazza.
Morning opens over the church
like a pale and holy visage.

I can see the place on the steps
where you stood yesterday
as light drew aside
the curtain of darkness.

I imagine your stance,
the way your hands hang loose
at your side like odd flowers,
the curve of your chin

catching the dawn,
and how your eyes drift
like fog across the valley,
how today you vanished

like a lost bird. My hands
shake from the cold, emotion,
or the cup of Arabica,
a small white anchor
for my ship of sorrows.

Lines to Gregory Corso
Protestant Cemetery, Rome

Taking a photo of Shelley's shrine,
I notice you on the ground
in a square of marble, asleep
among little beards of grass.

Genuflecting there, surprised,
I imagine your bones beneath,
with one hand raised in greeting, or
your skeletal arms linked with Shelley's
in some subversive subterranean pact,
with Keats looking on from the next quadrant.

A Roman pilgrimage brought
my aching feet to your resting place,
to read your verse of sorts, shorter
and more wistful than the rest,
shawled in silent ivy,
fingered by a sprig of blue wisteria
no bigger than a cigarette butt.

Did you think of joining your mother,
who left you as a baby on the Lower East Side
to seek these ancient temperate hills,
or was it simply your last wish to recline
near the one who flew like a skylark
into the west wind?

Let the Tiber remind me
of all your quirky songs
shrouded in cigarette smoke,
the odd fragmented verses
rendered stoned and eloquent
from the sofas of friends.

At the Protestant Cemetery

The sky presses heavy over Rome,
a bell jar of autumn humidity. Still,
cafes are crowded, coffee and *biscotti*
prevail. Blackbirds scavenge
the plane trees, their chatter
a darkling song.

The tram trundles its human load
past chiseled saints and gods
muscled in marble. In the graveyard,
Corso curls up near Shelley,
with Keats a neighbor.
They lie in wait for lightning to bloom
on a cloud, for thunder to shake
the limpid ivy, the last purple
wisterias glowing incandescent
like odd fireflies.

I make this poem for you,
the cat on the stone steps,
and for you, Gregory, Prince of Beats,
and you, John, who died of wasting sickness,
for whom autumn
is always a woman in love,
and you, blithe Percy, who joined
the wet waves of darkness too soon,
unready for Neptune's lust
or the sky's full-bodied rain
this dark afternoon.

Letter from Italy

Last night at Trevi Fountain,
four deep take photos:
lovers pose before mammoth
marble. Nearby,

a priest at Santa Maria della Vittoria
drones the rosary, the chanting
of veiled women hiding Santa Teresa's
ecstasy, her wild stone robes.

Night brings souvenir-sellers
spreading leather and scarves
on sheeted cobblestones until
blue lights signal police.

A full moon spells memories
of Cousin Rosetta's kitchen,
six hours south, where the family
gathers for pasta and eggplant,

local cheeses, miraculous meats.
Crossword puzzles in Italian and English
pepper the night with random words.
Our foreign tongues peck the air

like sparrows hungry for seed,
echo over laundry on the balcony,
fall like sweet figs from Tonino's tree,
ready for eating.

Outside Rome

life limps along
without crowds and Michelangelo.
Graffiti is the conversation here,
stray dogs, trams, markets
with Moroccan leather and shoes
made in China.

No fountains or miracles
except the *pasticceria* next door,
where espresso is the dark flower
of morning and an apricot tart
blessed with powdered sugar
the liturgy of the day.

At night, the moon looks on
as ordinary people spill from buses,
flood the broken sidewalks
with footsteps and tired voices,
jingle keys and consonants
hidden in the deep pockets
of vowels.

Trastevere sleeps
with bread as a pillow.

Going to Paris

One day in the unforgotten future,
I will lie down on my bed alone
and commend my soul to God,
whose existence I have doubted
ever since I can remember.

I will close my eyes and wait for the light.
Someone will come in eventually—
the police, or a curious neighbor,
and be driven away by the stench of decay,
but not before finding on the night table
two pennies for the eyes
and a little jar half-full of morphine.

Meanwhile, I'll have dreamt
of an apartment in Paris
on a boulevard lined with trees
smelling of springtime—
Saint-Germain-des-Prés, just blocks away
from where, on a Wednesday, long loaves
of still-warm bread heave among
the market stalls, promising life.

On the Seine, boatloads of tourists
drift past the painters and booksellers,
waving at spires, distant bells,
cafés and fresh peaches,
smiling into the churning tide,
while I dance invisibly
through the Musée de Cluny, then
tumble into a summer carnival
at the Tuileries.

Varda, Train Station

No use crying for what used to be,
a station full of people
with someplace to go—
a grandmother in Croatia, a business lunch
in Budapest, the city of all longing.

Cracked windowpanes stare sightless
at the tracks' blind sweep.
They tell a story in a lost language,
with tongues of dust and weeds,
abandoned farms, the cemetery
overgrown, the church splintered
by lightning, its belfry fallen through
the tinderbox roof.

We said our goodbyes long ago
amid the shorn hayfields,
the pens of spotted pigs,
the gnarled elms and tin-roofed sheds.
Goodbye, little village of unhappy accidents.

I saved a stone from the road out.
It shines like glass when held to the sun,
like crystal when cupped by the moon.
No station left, but a long-winded whistle,
the screech of brakes on steel. Together they call,
"We are the way out. Come."

The Cousins' Visit

For the first time
we'll meet them on Mancunian terrain.
Pubs and ale. Sooty industrial streets.
And the sad-eyed sheep on the hill,
wet and somnolent.

We will greet them at the airport,
kiss them on both cheeks,
feed them tea and scones
with jam and cream while they long
for strong coffee in little cups.

Our clipped syllables will leave them
stunned and tired at the end of the day.
We'll make them shiver in the Pennines,
climb the Yorkshire dales, gloved and woolied.

Later, rubbing our hands at the fireplace,
we'll have bubble and squeak for supper,
or sausages made from the local pigs,
and sherry trifle in a big glass bowl.

Every night for a week,
while we kick off the bedclothes,
our Anglo-Saxon bodies engines of heat,
they'll huddle together under blankets,
beached, salty and brown in their dreams
of some Tyrrhenian shore.

After days of umbrellas and a grey stone sky,
plodding through castles and gorse on the moors,
they'll return to the land of wine, sun,
and vowels like tangled linguini.

We'll ask them to remember us
every time it rains.

Easter 2013, Scotland

Picture a farmer crying.
He wears Wellington boots,
a woolen cap and gloves,
a coat against the wind.
He holds a spade. His breath
surrounds his face
in an aura of whitish death.
He has just uncovered
another lamb.

The newspaper reports
thirty-five-foot drifts
in the Highlands, where
newborn lambs have frozen
in mounds, small corpses
limp and scarcely distinguishable
from the ever-falling white.

Windblown dunes sift
among the rills, the downs
where ewes have birthed
then scattered shivering
into grottos.

Where is
the Lamb of God
that haunts these hills at Easter,
sacrificial but tidy in the prayerbooks?

The Good Shepherd has left
his flock, his staff and rod
back at the Psalms. David,
a shepherd boy turned
giant-killer and king,
never knew such sorrow

as that of the farmer
who swallows tears
as he shovels, who cradles
in his arms the tender lumps
of life, frozen hard as little
statues carved in ice.

Murder at the Palace Theatre

The rain spills
on the conservatory roof
like a broken necklace of pearls.
An enormous dark cloud wedges itself
into the hills as we step out
in the strange yellow light
of gilded puddles.

By the time we get to the theatre,
our umbrellas close uselessly
in our hands. The system has moved away,
and taxis hiss past us on damp roads
as night hunches towards curtain time.

Agatha Christie gives us murder tonight,
and to our delight, solves everything
in two hours with a minimum of violence
and a modicum of propriety.
The usual cast, from butlers to artists,
from would-be lovers to impossibly rich uncles,
emerges from velvet drapes to smile and bow,
their vengeance forgotten
in the glare of colored lights.

After such white-gloved cleverness,
crowds mill about on the sidewalk,
then click off towards the parking garage,
breathless in the warm gusty winds,
a respite before midnight thunder
shivers them in their pajamas
throughout the quilted night.

PART III
Objects of Desire

Mortality

I learned at school
that matter can neither be created
nor destroyed, but merely changed
from one form to another.

One fingerprint, different from
all others, will join sweat, snowflake,
breath, ice, wind, become
the electrical charge of lightning.

I am the profound humidity,
you the darkened sky. Together we
will provoke the purple clouds
to flash gold, a momentary
epigram for us.

We discuss this over coffee.
I watch the physic of your breath,
the geography of your face,
the marvelous mechanism of your hands
holding the cup, peeling an orange.

We will surely live forever
on the edge of reality, spirit-stems
blooming invisible buds.
How vicious death would be if final,
the coup-de-grâce of all
our useless gatherings.

Smoke

Nowhere to breathe
in the still-smoky parlor,
windows stuck shut
watching our claustrophobia
with closed eyes.

Each closet holds a life
of towels, sheets, clothes
holey with cigarette burns.
Someone says it's a miracle
the house never burned down.

Smoke whispers away
any thought of ventilation,
hushes the upholstery
into a brown funk.

Breezes never entered here,
nothing now to soothe
the raw wounds of grief
and the burning throats of mourners,

the family consigned
to cleaning the house,
down to the last ashtray,
the last pile of cold-embered stubs,
the walls flushed with nicotine,
his parting gift to the world.

Living Room

The grimy mirror
above the fireplace
reflects a life
spent in an armchair
with a can and a cigarette.

At the old house, we lift
too carefully
the pictures off the wall—
weddings, the Pope,
a collection of miniature
spoons under glass.

White rectangles
loom like ghosts
from nicotine walls,
shining through
a residue of smoke.
Carpet fibers stiffen
in the yellow glow.

The television will go
to the scrap-yard.
Muscled men,
surly as the day is damp,
haul away sofas,
rip up rugs, discard
the dead weight
of old mahogany.

Advent

Hands can catch
water from a stream

for drinking or the gathering
of stones, or the feel of something

cold, pure, elemental.
Grasping the dark is harder.

Winter's rough air
slips through outstretched fingers.

Un-embraceable night
fills with wisps of wanting,

thoughts of old lovers, the dead
and dying, falling through space.

Our open palms hold only
lamentations. We await

the promise of fire, receive only
darkness,

and bow under it, bow to it,
the unseen star.

god is

a pitiable thing,
a rabbit limping in the garden,
collapsing into the sedum.

god is a reminder
of what heaven forgot—
what?

god is the space under the stairs
where one hides from tornadoes,
or bombs in wartime.

god is the trampled leaf,
the frosted nub of bud,
alive and dying all at once.

god is a mirage in the desert,
where the camel comes to drink
and finds nothing but sand.

god is a way of being alone,
of reading a poem while dreading
the distance ahead.

god is the footprint one follows
to find the old aunt, the dead uncle
in the photograph.

god is the Acheron boatman
who ferries passengers
into the flaming dark.

I have waited all summer
to don the dress I adore,
the one with the yellow flowers
spelling g-d.

notes to god

make me the earth
that turns in your plough

make me lettuce and lavender
bake me into a pomegranate pie

make me the white dwarf star
that burns itself out

a cube of sugar dissolving in tea
cobalt wings in a cobalt sky

candy more lonely than sweet
shield me from a leprous moon

a dying sun   show me
flower and thorn

teach me how to be lost
some day this page

will be thicker than my bone
so set me to sail

in a glass-bottomed boat
through which you appear

gliding like a timeless
gleaming fish

Still

I teach my Italian cousin
two meanings for "still"—
"as always," and "without movement."

Still here, I say, though we
could die any time at our age.
We think of this at the cafe,

sometimes aloud.
The inexplicable benediction
of some faceless God

will decide when and who
submits to the scythe. Meanwhile,
we ponder how to let the sun

enter in as before,
let the rain and the hills
keep on feeding the soul.

On the piazza
pigeons peck at crumbs.
Their iridescence flits

between black and green
with violet silks. Tourists
come and go like so many sailboats

dotting the lake. How to be still
as the harbor at dawn, to remain
unmoved and unmoving,

the still life of a bowl of fruit,
of the mountain in whose shadow
we speak?

Quiet House

Easy to think of death these days
while brewing tea, reading the newspapers,

walking up a long hill. Years ago,
it never would have occurred to me

to obsess over the approaching end,
a cold blade on an innocent neck.

Depressing, friends would say,
like watching a sad film at the cinema

alone with one's popcorn.
Intimate morbidity has crept

into the room where the fireplace
grows cold, constellations hover

over chimneys, a book lies open
face down on the night-table.

On the hard ground outside,
spent tulips shed crimson skins,

still juicy for a time,
even without their heads.

In the kitchen, a half-filled kettle,
a lifted latch on the door.

Bells

Like cupped hands,
dark caves, or the dome
of sky, bells give and take
the gift of space, holding
in their mouths the wordless
language of resonance.

How would their tongues utter
lamentation or joy, funeral or wedding,
if not for the space that welcomes
breathless echoes and eschews
the claustrophobia of muffled things.

It's air they treasure,
the perfect rest for the clapper's bronze
which asks only the room to move
within the iron heart of emptiness,
to flail about until it can no more.
The miracle of sound, conceived in void
and birthed in the clarity of metal on metal,

soars above ropes and the frail ringers
lifted off their feet to play the changes.
Blessing the belfries, it drifts like smoke
down to the village of dreams.

Bodycolour

William Havell, 1782-1857
Cilgerran Castle, Pembrokeshire, Wales

The museum guide explains
that "bodycolour" is gouache,
the gleaming excess of pigment
that sets the stones aglow
with a white fire wherever
the painter wants kindling.

I imagine Havell
eating cheese and bread, staring
at the empty quarter-sheet of paper,
scratching his balding pate,
wondering where to put a castle
the size of a thumbnail, a black sliver
of boat, a whole river rushing
to swallow itself in the palm of God.

I can hear his pencil tap,
a swift outline, the unthinking calligraphy
of peak and crag, castle and canoe,
the bony outline of shore,
the empty space of river
at the heart of things.

Did he choose ochre then
to wash the page in old sunlight,
a castle's yellow ruins
asleep in a golden sky,
then add daubs of blue and green
following the tensile fragments
of deciduous dreams? After that,
he must have fallen asleep
in his studio over a tankard of ale,
miniature brush in hand, and dreamt
of nothing but where to trail the reds tomorrow
where the reeds echo the gnats' cantata.

The critics found his light too bright,
but even at the end, he needed that,
needed the brilliant skies at morning,
bleeding juices of fallen fruits,
the biblical streams of light
rolling like smoke over the valley,
a cowherd's shoulder aglow,
the wet nose of the spaniel.
He needed that last dab of sun,
even as he needed bread, cheese,
and ale, even as he breathed
finally into the dark.

Reading Garcia Lorca in Italian

The poems of Garcia Lorca
lurk deckle-edged and yellow
in a used bookstore in Tucson.
Someone from Siena once turned
crisp pages, then crossed an ocean,
donned cowboy boots, rode in
on a ghost horse to leave the book
at the rim of the Arizona desert
for some unknown lover of words.

The labyrinth of dual languages
beckons darkly. I choose the rope of Italian,
letting the Spanish drift away. A few words
flutter bat-like from the edge of Seville
to the seven hills of Rome: love, crystal,
balconies, lanterns, light.

L'albero di sangue—the tree of blood.
Garcia Lorca once stood before the firing squad
years after he wrote of the children
of Cordoba and journeyed to New York
to recover from madness
and watch Wall Street crumble.

Mid-page where one poem ends,
the word *ausilio*—"help"—
has been crossed out twice
among cypresses and birds.
Three pencil sketches of an ant,
or some segmented insect the size
of my thumb, scuttle below.

The Italian word for "tremble" precedes
the phrase *Come sei sola nella tua casa
vestita di bianco?*—"Why are you home
alone dressed in white?" and then,
dispensing with formalities,
E come difficile dirti: Io t'amo—
"And how difficult to tell you:
I love you."

A strip of dark pink taffeta
embroidered in flowers with the word
Seguimi—"Follow me"—has been
imprisoned among the gypsy songs
for half a century by whoever held this tome
decades ago, loving *crepuscolo*, the dawn,
those cold hours when one reads,
sleepless, in the dark, dreaming of Granada.

See-Saw at Dusk

yellow sign   two silhouettes
children play   in the deepening night

the ground of being   vanishes
every half minute

and for a nanosecond
both are stilled   in the darkening air

they face   each other
hanging on   brightly

find   their own way
of balancing   feet dangling

then down firm   for the push
electricity's in the air   overhead

wound tight   inside
crossed wires   telephone poles

nearly obsolete   oh to rise
with no   moorings

vertical   faith
horizontal   hope

diagonal   crossings
gravity   gone

the rusty   streak
separating   then joining

they pivot
even the fulcrum   floats

one up   one down
don't   jump off

just
yet

Sidewalk and Ball

Far from the sea,
the unmeasured distance
of flower and sky,
a red rubber ball
sidles the cobblestones.

Some random thrust of foot or hand
brought stone and toy together
as evening caught its breath
while waiting for a burst of crimson.

Leaving the sidewalk unfinished,
sweat-stung masons have taken
their muscled hands home
to hold beer and bread.

The children have been called in
for dinner, their sticky fingers
now soaped under a faucet.
Children prefer happiness to milk.

Tomorrow promises a finished
pavement, cemented in small squares
inch by patient inch. The jot
of red joy flung on concrete
is rediscovered, thrown hand to hand
out of the laborers' way, dancing
into the middle distance,

while stars hide their bright heads
in the pillows of morning,
and another day comes bounding
through Berlin.

Saxophone Quartet

An old indoor market in Berlin
features the music of four bleating sheep
dressed in brass: a throaty chorus
over a tangle of cords, shoes at eye level.

Four holes, empty of what
they had held only yesterday:
A purple glove, a green flower,
a yellow plum, a red sky. From each
echoes another texture—feather,
snow, clay, silk. In form, the same letter "J,"
a caterpillar coiled on a leaf.

From one bore emerges a landscape of solitude,
another strange food from the sky, the third
shoals of silver fish. The fourth, blind in one eye,
sings of her own affliction.

The holes are full of humanity
spilling out invisibly. North,
south, east and west, as the wind
blows. Paper, scissors, rock,
and something else unnamable.
Earth, air, fire, water.

The cyclamen in the window box
across the city vibrates. A wine glass
trembles behind grey shutters.
Sound in the shape of a question mark
holds the stars and all their messages,
burns my throat, settles in my chest
like a lump of gold.

Piccolo

No one wants the piccolo.
Sorting out my life, I discovered in the closet
a sterling bird known to shriek three octaves
and crown a Sousa march,
or rest for a hundred tacit bars of a symphony
in the lap of the second chair flute.

It's been years since my querulous embouchure
kissed the warbler's beak,
my breath exploring his tubular mysteries,
but now my lips, like the rest of my body,
sag and groan. And no one wants to buy
my piccolo, that silver lark
whose incessant chirps once pierced the cosmos.

Little tyrant of youthful songs,
hot as curry, strong and tensile
as the wire holding Wallenda,
it cuts the sky like a comet on an August night.
But no one wants to buy a shooting star.

How Things Go

At the open rehearsal of *The Rite of Spring*,
the waves from Lake Michigan roar
beyond the park, the giant seashell of a pavilion
gathering symphony and tide together
in a net of echoes.

Later, at home, the tree-trimmers arrive.
They are now asleep on the grass,
but for the first four hours they shimmied
up the Norway maple on ropes,
sliced dead growth off the linden,
shaved the crabapples, screwed a bolt
into the Autumn Blaze against
winter's icy crack.

The lawn is strewn with corpses
of leafy green, sacrificed
to the gods of fertility, like Stravinsky's
virgin who has just danced herself to death
in a park in Chicago.

And what will take you and me,
the dance or the saw, the dervish
or the deadpan buzz? This day,
we give ourselves over
to the song of the cellos,
the lopping of limbs, the drum's steady throb,
the final gong reverberating over the lake,
our old bones not yet ready for sleep.

Only Connect

I must play piano now

                                       but first
the fingernails must go

                 the clicking on the keys
is annoying and besides

                     one must fully touch
                                   ivory
with the pads of the fingers

                 to send weight from the shoulder
                      pull sound
                 from the innards of ebony

don't envy
         the talons of women
                 carefully glossed red and black
                     coy pinks
or the French manicures
                 of the idle

one must shed the little vanities
            with ease
      enter the music
             with no regrets

At the Museum

The statues are breathing across
a dust-moted afternoon, across centuries.
The window frames what's left of the city.
The sidewalk speaks no syllables,
basks in the grandeur of old colonnades.
The sky's gray body settles
into its own threadbare coat.

Sometimes the locals find shelter here,
shivering in fleece and wool,
seeking old friends among the pedestals,
watching for a piece of themselves in marble
or stone, a saint among Byzantine mosaics
who offers a modicum of comfort
in a world smelling of exhaust fumes
and yesterday's coffee.

The dregs of life are cupped outside
in a gust of wind, in a busload of tourists.
Inside the careful humidity of art,
multiple forms in flesh or plaster,
in blood, bone or pigment, mingle,
predisposed to warmth, wondering
what on earth they will do

at closing time, when blinking lights
mandate disconnection, when clicking reds
of security replace the rhythmic beats
purpling through the human heart.

Sleep

"...that knits up the raveled sleave of care..."
—Shakespeare

Cradled in the dark sea
of dreams, we taste a little death
each night. We cannot live

without this temporary coma,
a tentative excursion to the nether,
an orientation to starlessness,

a private preview of nonexistence.
We dissolve in the fusty breath
of evening, awaken soon

to sparrowsong, pollendust,
lavender air, in the disappearing
arms of the moon.

The lark's song weds
the curlew's cry at sunrise,
abandoning the studded sadness

of dreams. Sleep makes us whole
with each axial turning
around the sun's incandescent orb.

We join again the cortege
of the living dead, chanting
our ghostly songs at dawn.

PART IV

Lost Habitat

The Pines

To watch the evergreens felled
amid the terrible sound of saw
is today's definition of sorrow.

Even the ropes mourn, coiling their misery
around a neighboring maple,
pulling the hapless pines earthward.

We'd planted the green flames years ago,
named them Faith, Hope and Charity.
We'd had such faith in their feathered virtue,

the hope of things to come, the sturdy love
of outstretched arms shading summer's
drought-stricken earth, awaiting bird

and snow in equal measure. Now we celebrate
the mysteries of desire and death.
How were we to know

Austrian pines draw pests, bleed
poisoned sap white-clotted
on blistered trunks, drop needles

that graze the would-be grass
with the prickles of incipient death.
The truck-bed is piled high

with the mulch of the deceased,
and space weighs heavily against the sky.
Stillness, the Zen of zero.

Tomorrow,
the grinding of the stumps.

Extinction

Reading about dead buds
in the morning papers—
also a dying breed—
I listen to the rustle
of newsprint, smell the ink,
grainy on the page,
and suddenly feel in my fingers
the greenness of ferns
caught in the reflection
of the narrow-leaved hellebore.
The field scabious,
the yellow rattle,
and cranesbills in Northumbria
once roamed roadside and valley,
the round-fruited rush
in Gloucestershire,
and all the species
of orchids, coral and purple,
killed in Sussex.

Institutional hacks
with mowers and goggles
extinguish small flowers
in their prime. The now-
homeless orange-tip butterfly
seeks somewhere to light
near Chudleigh, among
the garlic mustard
by the train station,
little friends abandoned
in a cloud of herbicide.
Folding the newspaper,
I hear the near-extinct
crinkle of page on page,
and go out for a walk
around the reservoir
to find a bit of clover
not yet withered
in the April grass.

Mountain and Lake

The mountain must have come first,
the lake once a glacier slicing stone

with an irrevocable blade of ice.
Then the melt lay siege,

witness to this gentle panorama
born of a thousand small wounds.

Now the lake crouches
in the shelter of granite and grove,

having surrendered her ancient sword
into the hands of the hill.

Lake without mountain, uncontained,
would rush over the harbor

and vanish into crystal.
Mountain without lake would regress

to naked beast, with nothing to hold
in its rocky grasp, full of the emptiness

of its own grandeur. Together, transfixed,
they need no purpose under the moon.

Summer's Lease

The honeyed buzz of locusts
wrings desire from the night's
dark wanting. Cradled
in summer, too hot to sleep,
they enter the rubbing of wings.

Soon, in the frost's fierce grip,
the cabbage moths will cease
scrubbing the white-hot moon
and leave the flame-blooded darkness
in the hands of dead trees.

Regret is a fallen leaf,
a wing stuck on a window.
The frozen silks of winter
will soon unravel from the sky,
their pale skeins rustling.

Hedges

The hedges have needed
pruning for some time,
craving the blades
of rusted shears,
the freshness of trimmed twigs
and raw branches that heal
in the sweetest of seasons.

Hedges thrive on violence,
love the happy hand
that cuts them down,
the oftener the better,
wielding edges sharp
as the song of the lark.

Cut now. You've hesitated
long enough. Bring on
the young green of spring
that always sprouts and sings
and never dies.

The Long Hill

On the brow, briefly abandoned
by golfers and dogs, the war monument
rises in the distance.

Just twenty minutes ago
we were there. Our phantom
presence hovers overhead.

The foggy brambles
become open fields, lambent-green,
moist underfoot, and below,

cows graze at a thumb-sized dairy.
We tread the narrow lanes,
muddy gravel crossed by runnels
and a stile or two, then whisper

into the woods where oak leaves
spread their ruined gold.
Winding up the ribs of the hills,

we emerge into the sky itself,
which holds the many years
we've plodded here.

The pub at the top has closed,
a ghost of wattle and thatch.
Up here among the hedgerows,

dry stone walls, barbed-wire pastures,
the glow of a light in a far-off cottage,
red double-decker buses

wobbling through the village below,
what's left to say about
the passage of time?

River

Each year is another bend in the river.
Only the opposite shore is visible.

The water reflects sky, cloud, boat,
pleated by small exhalations of wind.

Once a year we meet
the cousins from another country.

We concoct magical reunions
oceans from reality.

The course of the water eludes
sight and sense, forces us to imagine

what lies beyond.
We know somehow

the future drifts in the river,
its serpentine hands, its Medusa-hair

coiling through the valleys,
far from the tranquil pier.

Stormy

Strange how childhood
comes flooding back
when a newsworthy storm
lashes New Orleans,
and Lake Pontchartrain
becomes a cyclone.

I feel like a kid again,
a Yankee summering
with southern cousins
who wore coonskin caps
and shot BB guns
while squatting in trees.

My favorite things—
grape popsicles
that dyed my tongue purple,
frogs, but mostly
swimming in streets
brimmed with the backwash
of hurricanes while Aunt Betty
peeled sodden towels
off windowsills and lintels.

It always rained sideways
through the cracks,
like memories
intruding on an ordinary day:
driving to work,
picking up groceries, or watching
a dragonfly light on a leaf.

Storm after Drought

Last night, when rain stroked
the scarred earth, entering the cracks
with small invasive hands,
and clouds sang the cantos
of momentary loss, shaking the trees,

we lay in our beds breathless,
feeling relief creep through our bodies
feet first, like some mythical spell,
knowing we ought to love the sun,
but tired from the endless parching,

the oppressive blue, the colors
of fake happiness bearing down
with their false cheer. Now
we give thanks for the torrent,
the thunder, the dark.

Aftermath

Wires and water
don't go well together.
The hurricane has forced them
to cohabit streets filled
with floating debris,
lumber, children's toys,
a car, someone's stove
drifting by like a cloud
sauntering in a blue sky,
the kind of sky they haven't seen
for days in New Jersey.

They say that glaciers
are abandoning the Arctic,
taking their shadows with them,
the long dark streaks that follow
the sun. Playful winds jinx
the ocean to a fury,
making windup toys
of ocean liners at the pier,
casting cold charms from Canada
on the Gulf Stream that left home
in search of adventure
to find it in New York.

The tawdry tango of fire and water
becomes an unforgettable performance.
Uptown, a transformer,
seeking notoriety and glamour,
crackles in the chrysanthemum dark,
then moves the show to Cleveland,
where it tours the lake road,
cleaves a tree and downs it,
no tickets needed.

Fallen

The leaf, deckle-edged, heart-shaped,
lies between puddle and cracked pavement,
brown-rimmed, red at the core.

She cannot return to the tree, to the twig
that held her by a thin stem for so long,
to the branch that shadowed her tracery.

The wind has had its way with her.
A veined, fleshed survivor.
A lost valentine.

Rockery

The gardens have squandered their riches
on an early spring, and now lie withered
and spent. The heather, of course,
still laughs its happy lavender
beside pink camellias blanched in the rain.
Too early for the rhododendrons
to come clambering down the hillside,
raucous and wild. Mud smudges
the stone steps, the puddled paths
reflecting the nothing of a low sky.

Elated that it's not raining today,
we drive here through motorway chaos
and wedge the car inside the gate,
prepare for waterfalls of color. Instead,
the daffodils hang their heads shrunken and brown,
the cherry blossoms have dropped in yesterday's
downpour, and the gaudy primrose haven't yet
elbowed their way through the ferns.

In future, we will recall these walks,
some prettier than others. The exquisite call
of the blackbird, trapped in a nondescript body,
sings delight from some scented corner
of mossed rock. We stop to listen, unable to find
the focal point, the open beak.

Rapt in the gifts of the present moment,
we smell the dampness binding leaf and flower
to stone and ear. Tonight
we'll imagine a burgundy moon
spilling the azaleas red.

Dahlias

Today I looked at the photographs
of last summer's dahlias, brash faces
crowding a London garden with lemon
and magenta, a folly of profusion.

How I needed those deep colors
turning to the sun, breaking through
the pinpoint English rain with a sudden brilliance,
licking stone walls with luminescence.

Here in Chicago, a colorless winter
prevails, the days sickly and mild,
waiting for snow. White would silence
everything—the dull lawns brown-stippled,
leftover asters, bits of newsprint stuck in shrubs,
while the whole world beyond dies
in blizzards unforeseen.

Something in this global garden
is amiss. Geese stagger into traffic.
Birds have forgotten to migrate—
I can hear their idle chirpings in the dawn.

It seems just yesterday
that small, fat English robins
fluffed out their ruby breasts
among the willows, swallows swarmed
over scissortail meadows and, awaiting
the certain death of the hoarfrost, dragonflies lit,
iridescent, on dahlias that could not decide
whether to be purple or red.

Robin

A great flash
of pentecostal wings

descending russet breast black unblinking eyes

she ravishes intruders those lawn-waterers and

petunia-weeders who threaten
her nest unconscious of

the silent chorus of beaks
protruding from the basket

of twigs, singing "mother"

from atop
the linden
tree

Noncommittal

Tonight Jupiter will rise
to the upper right of the moon,
and tomorrow, Venus will join them,
low and luminous in the east.

The earth below, that piteous planet
of floods and wars, mudslides and fires,
cracks from the drought in our small corner
of Midwest America. Thirst travels
from the bottom of each crevasse
in the yellowing yards to the surface
packed like cement.

This is the story of heaven and earth,
each consumed with its own domain,
and of life in between, of six billion humans
conceived in sweat and desire,
the hydrangeas fanning themselves,
the dying plucking at the bedclothes,
the dancers at the barre
with their blistered feet tied up in old satin,
all in their parallel orbits.

Try to remember
this week Venus will ascend
from horizon into heaven.

Grapes

The grapes are heaped
in a glass bowl, green,
red and bruised purple
clustered in bundles,
languorous over the lip,
their powdery patina
like grandmother's jewels.

If they could talk, they'd speak
the language of earth's hot star,
of poisons, calloused hands
plucking from vines the globed
unfermented beauty trucked
to markets, the exhausted tale
of too-brief lives.

Just yesterday they seem
to have shrunk, their fine skins
withered, losing luminosity,
still embracing each other
in their last hours, sweeter
than sweet becoming rot,
greener than grass, deeper
than the crimson sky
presaging the storm.

The sky is falling in
on vineyards, bent backs,
shacks and trailer parks
where pickers sleep on shelves
and children never learn to read.

In an air-conditioned bar,
we linger over garnet goblets,
observing our own wrinkled skins,
our intimate selves gathered together
for the last sip of wine.

Only because

it's the longest day
I write a poem, uninspired
by the long drought, the cracked earth,
the drooping hydrangeas, the parade
of black ants I've never seen before
crossing the front steps, the yellow
grass crisp underfoot, the sparrows
bathing in dust, flailing their wings.

At night the Dipper is empty,
holding nothing but a void
of stars. I await rain
from this most unlikely source,
imagining it tip and pour,
drenching the evening sky.

Matter rearranges itself,
readying for tomorrow's storm,
forecast in red. Startled by thunder,
I drink the last electric years
from my cupped hands,

watch the moon's effervescence
turn my flesh to ash
in the first tentative drops.
From this moment, the days
will be foreshortened,
heading toward snow
and the still-beating of wings.

The secret of stillness

is elusive,
how the lilies cling to staunch stems,
how the roses, brown-edged
from the drought but uncomplaining,
let their heads droop gently down,
their hips holding them firm
until their last moisture
surrenders to the sun's avarice,

how the robin chews the worm,
the rabbit simply listens
to the wind, how the wind itself
subsides before the tempest
comes wheeling from the north,

how the oak tree sits like a castle
hundreds of years old, how the ship
barely moves on the horizon, how
the horizon swallows it without
motion, how the stars mark their paths
with invisible ink, how ink dries up
in the pen after the last poem.

Donna Pucciani was born in Washington, D.C., grew up in New Jersey, graduated *magna cum laude* from Marywood University with a degree is music, and earned an M.A. and Ph.D. in Humanities from New York University. She taught in secondary schools and colleges in the East and Midwest for several decades before retiring to write full-time.

Her poems have been published on four continents, translated into Chinese, Italian and Japanese, and nominated several times for the Pushcart Prize. She has won awards from the Illinois Arts Council, the National Federation of State Poetry Societies, Poetry on the Lake, Poets and Patrons of Chicago and other organizations. A resident of Chicago and Manchester (England), she served for many years as Vice President of the Poets' Club of Chicago.

Pucciani's previous books of poetry include *The Other Side of Thunder* (Flarestack, U.K., 2006); *Jumping Off the Train* (Orchard House Press, Washington, 2007); *Chasing the Saints* (Virtual Artists Collective, Chicago, 2008); *To Sip Darjeeling at Dawn* (Virtual Artists Collective, Chicago, 2011); and *Hanging Like Hope on the Equinox* (Virtual Artists Collective, Chicago, 2013).

CPSIA information can be obtained at www.ICGtesting.com
Printed in the USA
LVOW06s0202121214

418477LV00007B/15/P